BATS, STICKS & RACKETS

MARY ELIZABETH SALZMANN

Consulting Editor, Diane Craig, M.A./Reading Specialist

A Division of ABDO

ABDO
Publishing Company

visit us at www.abdopublishing.com

Published by ABDO Publishing Company, a division of ABDO, P.O. Box 398166, Minneapolis, Minnesota 55439. Copyright © 2012 by Abdo Consulting Group, Inc. International copyrights reserved in all countries. No part of this book may be reproduced in any form without written permission from the publisher. SandCastle™ is a trademark and logo of ABDO Publishing Company.

Printed in the United States of America, North Mankato, Minnesota
062011
092011

Editor: Katherine Hengel
Content Developer: Nancy Tuminelly
Design and Production: Anders Hanson
Image research: Stacy Nesbitt
Photo Credits: Thinkstock (George Doyle), Shutterstock

Library of Congress Cataloging-in-Publication Data
Salzmann, Mary Elizabeth, 1968-
  Bats, sticks & rackets / Mary Elizabeth Salzmann.
    p. cm. -- (Sports gear)
  ISBN 978-1-61714-823-1
  1. Sporting goods--Juvenile literature. I. Title.
GV745.S34 2012
688.76--dc22

                              2010053047

SANDCASTLE™ LEVEL: FLUENT

SandCastle™ books are created by a team of professional educators, reading specialists, and content developers around five essential components—phonemic awareness, phonics, vocabulary, text comprehension, and fluency—to assist young readers as they develop reading skills and strategies and increase their general knowledge. All books are written, reviewed, and leveled for guided reading, early reading intervention, and Accelerated Reader® programs for use in shared, guided, and independent reading and writing activities to support a balanced approach to literacy instruction. The SandCastle™ series has four levels that correspond to early literacy development. The levels are provided to help teachers and parents select appropriate books for young readers.

Emerging Readers
(no flags)

Beginning Readers
(1 flag)

Transitional Readers
(2 flags)

Fluent Readers
(3 flags)

CONTENTS

What Are...

BATS, STICKS & RACKETS ?

Bats, sticks, and rackets are sports gear.

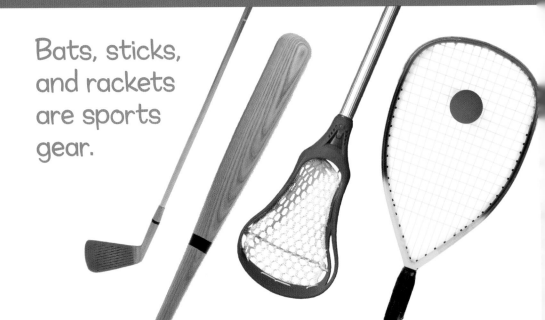

Players use them to hit things!

BASEBALL & SOFTBALL BATS

Baseball and softball players use bats to hit balls.

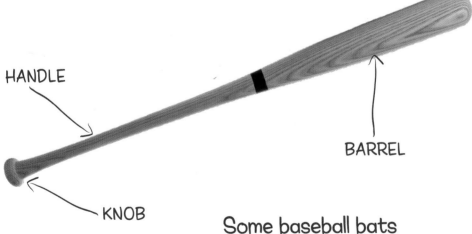

HANDLE

BARREL

KNOB

Some baseball bats are made of wood.

Softball bats are made of **metal**.

ICE HOCKEY STICK

Ice **hockey** players use hockey sticks to hit a puck.

The end of an ice hockey stick is called the blade.

BLADE

SHAFT

Players use hockey sticks to hit the puck into a **net**.

LACROSSE STICK

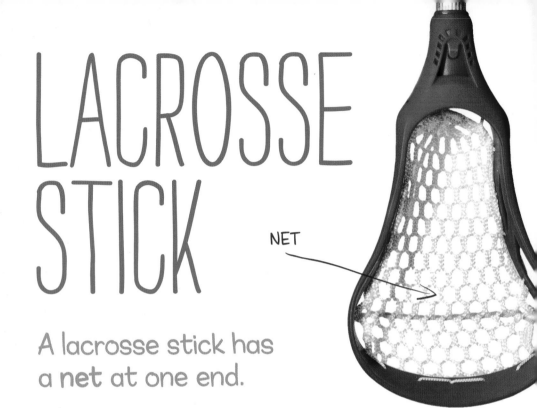

NET

A lacrosse stick has a **net** at one end.

A lacrosse player uses the net to catch and throw the ball.

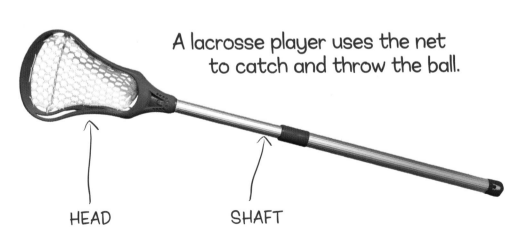

HEAD

SHAFT

GOLF CLUBS

Golfers use sticks called clubs.

Golfers use different clubs for different shots.

Wood   Iron   Putter

A putter is used when
the ball is close to the hole.

POLO MALLET

Polo players hit the ball with sticks called mallets.

The players hit the ball with the side of the mallet head.

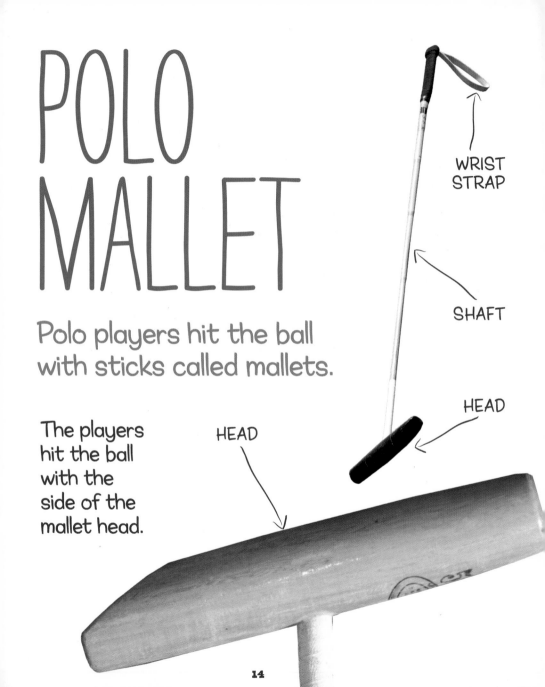

WRIST STRAP

SHAFT

HEAD

HEAD

A polo mallet is very long. A player can reach the ball while riding a horse!

RACQUETBALL &
TENNIS RACKETS

Tennis and racquetball players
use rackets.

HEAD

STRINGS

GRIP

RACQUETBALL
RACKET

TENNIS
RACKET

WRIST CORD

A racket head has strings **stretched** across it.

BADMINTON RACKET

Badminton players use a very light racket. The handle and **frame** are very thin.

Badminton players use the racket to hit a shuttlecock. A shuttlecock is also called a birdie.

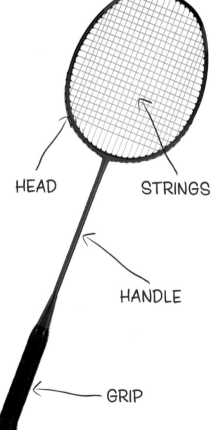

HEAD

STRINGS

HANDLE

GRIP

TABLE TENNIS PADDLE

Table tennis players hit the ball with a paddle.

HEAD

RUBBER

HANDLE

A table tennis paddle has a very short handle.

Most table tennis paddles are made of wood. There is rubber on one or both sides.

FUN FACTS

- Most wooden baseball bats are made of ash or maple.

- An ice hockey goalie's stick has an extra wide shaft.

- Each side of a table tennis paddle is a different color.

QUICK QUIZ

1. The end of an ice hockey stick is called the blade. True or False?

2. A putter is used when the ball is far from the hole. True or False?

3. Racquetball and tennis rackets have strings. True or False?

4. Badminton players use a very heavy racket. True or False?

GLOSSARY

frame – a border that surrounds something and holds it together.

metal – a hard, shiny substance such as iron or copper that is dug out of the earth.

net – a material, such as fabric or knotted threads, that is used to catch things.

stretched – pulled tight.